18 STITCHES OF LOVE

NILOY SHOUVIC ROY

This book, "**18 Stitches of Love**," is dedicated to myself and to all the lovers who have found healing through the power of love. It is a tribute to the resilience of the human spirit, the transformative journey of self-discovery, and the profound impact that love, in all its forms, can have on our lives. May this book serve as a beacon of hope and a reminder that love is the thread that mends our hearts and stitches our souls back together.

Contents

Foreword

Thank you to **Grammarly** and **Duplichecker** for their invaluable assistance in rectifying my grammatical errors and ensuring the originality of my work by checking for plagiarism. Your tools have been instrumental in refining my writing and maintaining the integrity of this book.

Preface

After experiencing a major heartbreak, I found myself on a path of self-destruction. The pain was so overwhelming that I turned to alcohol and cigarettes, consuming them in dangerous quantities in an attempt to numb my sorrow. My life spiraled out of control until one fateful day when an accident landed me in the hospital. I received 18 major and 6 minor stitches on my leg, a physical manifestation of the emotional wounds I had been carrying.

Lying in that hospital bed, I realized I had a choice: I could continue down this destructive path or harness the power of my broken heart for something positive. I chose the latter. I decided to bleed through my pen and write this book, channeling my pain and experiences into a story that might help others.

To all the broken lovers out there, I implore you not to destroy your life for someone who doesn't even care. It's important to wait and believe that someone will come along who will help heal the wounds you are enduring. As SRK said, *"I feel like the King of the world, aaj is baat ka bhi yaqeen ho gaya ki humare filmon ki tarah humare zindage mein bhi, end tak sab kuch theek ho jaate hai 'Happy Endings', aur agar theek na ho, toh woh the End nahi, picture abhi baaki hai mere dost."*

In writing **"18 Stitches of Love,"** I have poured my heart and soul into these pages. It is my hope that through my story, you find solace, strength, and the courage to believe in happy endings, even if they seem far away right now.

Acknowledgements

I am deeply grateful to my family and brothers, whose unwavering support and encouragement pushed me to write once more. Your belief in me has been a source of strength throughout this journey.

A special thanks to "Rosogolla." Because of you, I am healing again, and it is through your inspiration that I found the strength to write this book. This is my way of saying, "I love you."

Through this book, I have immortalized my love for family, brotherhood, and you. Thank you for being a part of this journey and for helping me transform pain into purpose.

1. FIRST STITCH

I don't trust any girl from your city anymore,
A fortress built from broken dreams and shattered lore.
Echoes of laughter once sweet, now bitter in the breeze,
A haunting melody that brings me to my knees.
I am sorry for the wall I've built, this ironclad defense,
A response to wounds so deep, a shield of cold pretense.
I'm not ready for love, a sentiment forlorn,
A heart once open wide now tattered and torn.
I fear the touch of tenderness, the whisper of a vow,
For every promise made to me is broken now.
A landscape of betrayal, a desert of despair,
Where every step I take reveals a memory's snare.
I fear to love again, to open up my soul,
For vulnerability has left me with a heavy toll.
Each beat of my heart, a reminder of the pain,
A symphony of sorrow that courses through my veins.
Once, love was a garden where vibrant flowers grew,
But now it's just a wasteland of withered hopes, subdued.
The smiles, the lies, the sweet deceit that danced upon your lips,
Have left my spirit fractured, a vessel full of rifts.
Your city holds no refuge, no solace for my grief,
Only shadows of a past that offers no relief.

The streets where we once wandered, now haunted in the night,
Ghosts of our moments linger, out of reach, out of sight.
I am sorry for the scars that time will never heal,
For the innocence that's lost, for the emptiness I feel.
I'm not ready for love, for the faith I can't restore,
I don't trust any girl from your city anymore.

2. SECOND STITCH

After losing all my hopes from love,
You showed me all the positivity,
A beacon in the endless night,
A dream of what my life could be.
I didn't know, whether it was true or false,
I just blindly jumped into it,
With a heart once torn, now seeking light,
A soul yearning to be lit.
You painted skies with hues of dawn,
Erased the shadows of my fears,
Whispered promises of forever,
Dried the remnants of my tears.
In your embrace, I found a haven,
A sanctuary from the storm,
But deep within, a silent question,
Is this warmth, or just a form?
Days turned into fleeting moments,
Wrapped in laughter, lost in dreams,
Yet a voice, so soft and distant,
Echoed doubts in silent screams.
For every smile you brought to me,
A shadow lingered in my heart,

Was this love a pure intention,
Or a play, a scripted part?
Blindly, I gave you all my trust,
Hoping faith would make it right,
But the deeper that I wandered,
The more I lost my sight.
Your touch, a gentle contradiction,
A promise, yet a fleeting breeze,
Leaving me in constant wonder,
If my heart you meant to seize.
And now, as dawn breaks through my sorrow,
I stand alone, in morning's glow,
With shattered dreams and silent echoes,
Of a love I'll never truly know.
After losing all my hopes from love,
You showed me all the positivity,
But in the end, a lesson learned,
In truth lies the greatest clarity.
I didn't know, whether it was true or false,
I just blindly jumped into it,
Now I rise from depths of shadows,
With a heart forever lit.

3. THIRD STITCH

I don't know how to love again,
Please tell me a way to love again.
In shadows deep, where sorrows blend,
My heart still trembles, fears contend.
You shared your pain, your silent tears,
A heart once whole, now gripped by fears.
I respect your feelings, tender, true,
In your brokenness, I see me too.
You said you were broken, and so am I,
Beneath this mask, a constant sigh.
That's why I want to give you love,
A fragile gift, like mourning dove.
To offer what you've never known,
A warmth, a light, a gentle tone.
Even though I know, deep in my core,
This path might leave me torn once more.
Yet here I stand, with heart in hand,
A weary soul on shifting sand.
For in your eyes, a glimmer bright,
A hope that whispers in the night.
To mend what's shattered, piece by piece,
To find in love a sweet release.

Though scars may deepen, wounds may bleed,
I'll plant this love, a fragile seed.
Knowing well, it may be vain,
That in the end, I'll feel the strain.
But for a moment, fleeting, brief,
We'll share a solace in our grief.
So take this love, so tender, frail,
In stormy seas, we set our sail.
Though destined for a tragic shore,
I'll love you still, forevermore.
And if I break, if shadows fall,
If echoes answer sorrow's call,
At least I'll know, within this pain,
That I had tried to love again.

4. FORTH STITCH

In the vast expanse where stardust forms,

The universe whispers in cosmic storms,

"Your evolution is my grand design,

Comfort, a fleeting dream in time."

I stand here, heart open wide,

Trusting in love, no need to hide.

With every beat, a vow is made,

To cast away the shadows, not to be afraid.

I am trusting in love again,

In every whisper, every refrain,

For in your eyes, I see the stars,

A promise that heals all past scars.

I'll try to be a partner true,

To walk beside, to grow with you,

In every dawn and setting sun,

Until our hearts beat as one.

So let the past dissolve like mist,

In the warmth of a lover's kiss.

For you, I'll strive, and I'll be bold,

In your arms, a new story told.

Forget the pains that once did last,

For with me, they're in the past.

Together, we'll craft a future bright,
Guided by love's eternal light.
The universe, with all its might,
Aligns our paths in the silent night.
And though the road may twist and bend,
My love for you will never end.
In evolution's grand embrace,
We'll find our sacred, loving place.
So trust in love, as I do too,
For my heart beats only for you.

5. FIFTH STITCH

Now, finally, we are dating,

Yet I've failed to gain your trust completely.

I know I'm a bit immature in love,

But trust me, darling, you are all I want.

I still remember our first meet,

How you ran towards me to hug me tight.

In that embrace, the world seemed still,

Our hearts began a rhythm, right and light.

Then came our first kiss,

A moment that lingers, a timeless tryst,

We exchanged our breath under the tree,

A whispering witness to our blossoming mystery.

Your eyes, deep pools of star-lit nights,

Spoke promises of love, of future sights.

In your gaze, I found a home,

A place where all my dreams could roam.

I know I falter, young in love's embrace,

Yet in your arms, I find my grace.

Each day, I strive to be the man you need,

With every heartbeat, I plant a hopeful seed.

Our journey, like a river, flows,

Through valleys of trust, where true love grows.

Hand in hand, we'll brave each storm,
In your warmth, I find my norm.
Forgive my flaws, my trembling start,
For you, my love, possess my heart.
With every sunrise, my promise renews,
To love you, cherish you, in all life's hues.
Now, finally, we are dating,
And though trust is a garden yet to bloom,
Believe in us, in what we're creating,
In your love, I find my room.
So here I stand, my heart laid bare,
Hoping you'll see my genuine care.
Immature in love, yet ardent and true,
My world, my soul, revolves around you.
Together, let's write our tale,
A story of love, that will never pale.
Through laughter, tears, and endless nights,
Our love will soar, reach new heights.
Now, finally, we are dating,
And with each step, closer we'll become,
For in your love, my heart keeps waiting,
To prove to you, that you're my only one.

6. SIXTH STITCH

Now suddenly your ex called,
With a voice from the past,
A ghost resurrected,
A shadow you thought had vanished.
You obeyed him,
As if I were never here,
As if my love were a mirage,
A fleeting whisper in the wind.
And put me into the blocklist,
Erasing me with a tap,
A digital exorcism,
Severing our fragile connection.
That broke my heart,
A crack echoing through silence,
An echo of sorrow,
Resounding in the hollow chambers of my soul.
I felt shattered,
Pieces of me scattered,
Across the cold, empty floor,
Fragments of a love story now forlorn.
My hands started trembling again,
Shaking with the weight of betrayal,

The ghost of our moments,
Now phantoms that haunt my restless nights.
You broke my trust,
A bond once unbreakable,
Now reduced to ashes,
Swept away by the winds of your whim.
I am left in the ruins,
A solitary figure,
Picking up the remnants,
Of a love that once bloomed with hope.
Now suddenly your ex called,
And with him, took you away,
Leaving me in the darkness,
Where our dreams used to play.

7. SEVENTH STITCH

If I had known the depths of sorrow I'd face,
If I had known the crushing weight of solitude,
I would have rejected the gift of a heart altogether.
All I yearned for was happiness,
To bring joy to you.
I desired your happiness,
But happiness with me—
Is that too much to hope for?
Once, we lived in a world of light and laughter,
Where each moment was a promise of forever,
Your eyes spoke of dreams intertwined,
And our love seemed endless, pure, and true.
Now, those dreams lie shattered,
Scattered like leaves in the harsh winter wind,
Each fragment a painful reminder,
Of the love that slipped through our fingers.
The nights stretch on, filled with suffocating silence,
The weight of your absence crushes my spirit,
The laughter that once filled our lives,
Now echoes as a haunting specter.
If I had known the depths of sorrow I'd face,
If I had known the crushing weight of solitude,

I would have rejected the gift of a heart altogether.
All I yearned for was happiness,
To bring joy to you.
I desired your happiness,
But happiness with me—
Is that too much to hope for?
Your absence is a wound that refuses to heal,
A chasm that no time can bridge,
The days blur into a monochrome haze,
Every moment a testament to your absence.
I search the night sky for comfort,
But the stars mock my pain,
Each twinkling light a distant echo,
Of a love that has faded into nothingness.
If I could turn back time, I'd hold you closer,
I'd cherish each fleeting second,
I'd never take our love for granted,
And maybe, just maybe, we'd still be whole.
But now, all I have are fragments of dreams,
And the relentless ache of a broken heart,
A life filled with what-ifs and regrets,
A sorrow that knows no end.
If I had known the depths of sorrow I'd face,
If I had known the crushing weight of solitude,
I would have rejected the gift of a heart altogether.
All I yearned for was happiness,
To bring joy to you.

I desired your happiness,

But happiness with me—

Is that too much to hope for?

The world moves on, indifferent to my pain,

But I'm frozen in a past that refuses to release me,

A prisoner of memories, a shadow of my former self,

Lost in the echoes of a love long gone.

Seasons change, but they hold no meaning,

For without you, every day is bleak,

A relentless cycle of pain and longing,

A never-ending storm of despair.

So here I stand, a ghost of who I once was,

Lost in the shadows of a love that's died,

If I had known the cost of having a heart,

I would have never wanted one at all.

If I had known the depths of sorrow I'd face,

If I had known the crushing weight of solitude,

I would have rejected the gift of a heart altogether.

All I yearned for was happiness,

To bring joy to you.

I desired your happiness,

But happiness with me—

Is that too much to hope for?

8. EIGHTH STITCH

Tell me everything was a prank,
That the whispers in the dark were just a joke,
A cruel, heartless jest,
And you both were only lying.
Please, say it wasn't true,
That you are still mine, and I am yours.
Tell me it was all a game,
That the tears I shed were misplaced,
A misunderstanding in the night,
And that your heart still beats for me,
Even now, as the shadows lengthen,
And the echoes of your laughter haunt my dreams.
Tell me that you love me too,
That these lonely days are but a phase,
A fleeting moment in our endless story,
And that soon, we'll find our way back,
To the warmth of each other's embrace,
To the sanctuary of our shared dreams.
Even though I don't want to,
Even though my heart screams in protest,
Let's at least try,
To tell each other a lie,

That we still love each other,
As we once did, in the days before the fall.
Tell me, please, that I'm not alone,
That the silence is a ruse,
And that in the quiet, you think of me,
Long for me, as I long for you,
For without you, the world is but a shadow,
A hollow echo of what once was.
Let's pretend, if only for a moment,
That the pain is an illusion,
A trick of the mind,
And that we are still bound together,
By the invisible threads of love,
That once tied our hearts as one.
Tell me everything was a prank,
A cruel, heartless jest,
And you both were just lying.
Say the words, even if they are false,
For in this web of deceit,
Perhaps we can find a semblance of solace.
Let's lie to each other, and to ourselves,
That we still love each other,
That the world has not shifted,
That the stars have not dimmed,
And that somewhere, in the tangled mess of our hearts,
There is still a spark, a glimmer of what once was.
For I love you,

Even though I don't want to,
Even though the pain is unbearable,
And the nights are long and cold.
Let's at least try,
To tell each other a lie,
That we still love each other,
And perhaps, in that lie,
We can find a truth,
That love, once given, never truly dies.

9. NINTH STITCH

The smile you gave me is really worth dying for.
I refuse to accept that you are not in my life anymore.
Your laughter, your touch, the way you'd look in my eyes,
Now all that's left are these silent goodbyes.
You cannot go back to someone who tore you apart,
Breaking my heart into a million pieces,
Leaving me with only these hollow creases.
I feel suffocated, my soul is aching,
Every breath without you, my being is breaking.
Anxiety grips me, a relentless storm,
My hands and feet tremble, as if an earthquake's born.
Nights grow longer, darkness more profound,
In the silence of the night, your absence resounds.
Every memory, a ghost that won't let me be,
A cruel reminder of what used to be.
Your voice, a phantom whisper in the breeze,
Brings me to my knees, begging for some peace.
Please, stop this prank, this nightmare you've spun,
Embrace me once more, let us be as one.
Hold me tight, dispel this sorrowful trance,
Say "I love you, it was all a prank."
But reality remains, a bitter, harsh truth,

No gentle hands to soothe, no sweet voice of youth.
I wander through days, lost and forlorn,
In a world devoid of the love we once adorned.
The smile you gave me was my guiding light,
Now plunged into eternal night.
The stars above, cold and distant,
Reflect the emptiness, the void, the persistent.
Yet still I wait, in this endless despair,
Hoping one day, you'll reappear.
But till then, I am but a shell,
A broken heart in a solitary hell.
Your love, a phantom limb I can't ignore,
The smile you gave me, worth dying for.

10. TENTH STITCH

I cannot take this anymore,
The weight of memories, the hollow ache,
So I have decided to feel your touch, your presence
By drowning in the warmth of alcohol's embrace.
Right now, after finishing two Old Monk,
The world blurs, and I feel you close,
As if you're holding me under the tree of Rabindra Sarovar,
Where shadows of our past come alive in the night.
I am reliving that night, a fragment of us,
When we were together, sitting on that worn bench,
The air thick with secrets and silent confessions,
My lips tracing your neck, the world outside forgotten.
Suddenly, the lights turned on,
A harsh reminder of our stolen moments,
Both of us startled, eyes meeting, and we laughed,
Our laughter an echo in the silence, a fleeting comfort.
I miss your odour, a scent that lingers in my dreams,
Haunting my waking hours with cruel tenderness,
I miss the touch of your hands, the way they grounded me,
Now I am adrift, a ship lost at sea without your anchor.
I miss your lips, a whisper of promises never kept,
The ghost of their softness haunts my skin,

I miss you, an ache that time cannot dull,
A void that alcohol can only momentarily fill.
I miss us, the "we" that no longer exists,
Fragments of our love scattered like ashes,
I am left to gather the pieces, futile and broken,
In the bottom of an empty glass, searching for solace.
I cannot take this anymore,
The weight of absence, the hollow ache,
So I have decided to feel your touch, your presence
By drowning in the warmth of alcohol's embrace.
But in the end, all I find is emptiness,
A dark abyss where your memory resides,
And I am left alone, under the tree of Rabindra Sarovar,
Chasing shadows of a past that will never return.

11. ELEVENTH STITCH

I miss your kisses,
The taste of your lips,
The odour in your breath,
A whisper in the mist,
A memory etched in the fog of my mind,
Where shadows linger and time stands still.
I miss your hug,
Where our heartbeats get synchronized,
A symphony of love,
A rhythm of souls entwined,
Now lost in the cacophony of a lonely night.
So now I am lighting up this cigarette,
Replacing your lips with nicotine,
A bitter substitute for the sweetness of you,
A futile attempt to bridge the void,
To feel your love again, if only for a fleeting moment.
Even though it is temporary,
By sacrificing 10 minutes of my life,
I find solace in the burn, the smoke,
The way it curls and fades,

Like the ghost of you.
After all, nothing makes sense in life without you,
Days bleed into nights,
And the sun rises only to mock my despair,
Each dawn a cruel reminder,
Of a world devoid of your touch.
The stars have lost their sparkle,
The moon its silver glow,
And the silence is deafening,
A testament to my grief,
An echo of your absence.
I wander through the remnants of our past,
Haunted by memories,
Chased by the specter of what was,
A prisoner of my own longing,
Bound by the chains of love and loss.
The scent of your perfume still lingers,
A phantom in the air,
Taunting me with its presence,
A cruel reminder that you are gone,
Yet forever near.
In the haze of smoke,
I see your face,
A mirage of what was,
A dream that slips through my fingers,
As I clutch at the remnants of you.
I miss the way your laughter filled the room,

A melody that soothed my soul,
Now replaced by the deafening silence,
The emptiness of your absence,
A void that nothing can fill.
I miss the way your eyes sparkled,
A light that guided me through the dark,
Now I am lost, stumbling,
Blind in the abyss of my sorrow,
Searching for a flicker of hope.
Each drag, each inhale,
A desperate attempt to recapture,
To relive a moment of our love,
Knowing it is futile,
Yet clinging to the illusion.
For in the depths of my despair,
I find a twisted comfort,
In the pain, in the longing,
In the memory of you,
And the cigarettes that burn like my heart.
So I light another,
And another,
Chasing the ghost of you,
Sacrificing pieces of myself,
In a futile bid to feel alive.
For nothing makes sense in life without you,
The world is a canvas of gray,
The colors faded,

The joy drained,
And I am but a hollow shell.
I miss your kisses,
The taste of your lips,
The odour in your breath,
I miss your hug,
Where our heartbeats get synchronized.
Now I live in the shadows,
A prisoner of my grief,
A wanderer in the night,
Searching for a glimpse of you,
In the haze of smoke and the ashes of my soul.

12. TWELFTH STITCH

In the recesses of my soul, a flicker of hope ignites,
At last, you returned, like a wanderer seeking respite.
I clung to faith, believing in your transformation,
Forgiving past transgressions, seeking reconciliation.
Yet shadows loomed large, unveiling the deceit,
Each vow broken, as you pursued deceit.
The same old pattern, etched in our narrative,
Your promises, hollow, leaving wounds abrasive.
Yearning for love, for a bond unblemished,
To alleviate your anguish, to be your solace cherished.
But all I found was a twisted game of manipulation,
Where I'm left to drown in the depths of desolation.
Was it too much to seek love's purity divine?
To craft a future where trust would intertwine?
Instead, I'm ensnared in a labyrinth of lies,
As you dance with demons, heedless of my cries.
My once-open heart now cloaked in fear's embrace,
Your betrayal etched deep, leaving little space.
Can I muster the strength to trust once more,
Or am I fated to endure this torment's encore?

So I implore you, halt this ruthless charade,
Cease to rend my heart, in darkness it fades.
For I'm uncertain if I can withstand the pain,
Of loving you, only to be shattered again.

13. THIRTEENTH STITCH

I tried my best to make you forget about your past,
To build a new world where shadows wouldn't last.
But every time I see you almost letting go,
One phone call or text from your ex makes my all efforts go in
vain,
Dragging us back to those memories again.
I really do love you, with all my heart,
Yet I see us falling apart.
I strive to mend the pieces of your broken trust,
But your eyes remain clouded with ancient dust.
I am not the same guy who traumatized you,
I am a soul who wishes to be your rescue.
I wish to hold you and make you feel safe,
To take you away from that darkened place.
Each day I offer you my love, pure and true,
Hoping it's enough to bring light to you.
But the shadows of his betrayal linger still,
In every whispered word, in every chilled thrill.
I watch as his ghost tightens its grasp,
Around your heart, with every painful clasp.

My hands tremble, helpless, unable to fight,
The echoes of a past that smother our light.
I am here, pleading, on bended knee,
Begging for a chance, just to make you see.
That my love is a beacon in your night,
A steady flame in your endless fight.
But his memory is a relentless tide,
Washing away the bridges I've tried to provide.
And though I love you more than words can say,
I fear I'm losing you to yesterday.
Each tear you shed cuts through my soul,
Making my heart feel unbearably cold.
For every step forward, we take two back,
Lost in the labyrinth of what we lack.
I am not the man who caused your pain,
But my efforts to heal seem all in vain.
I stand here, loving you, broken and true,
Wondering if I'll ever reach you.
For every kiss, every promise I make,
Is shadowed by the trust he did break.
And though I give my everything to you,
It's never enough to erase what he put you through.
So I'll continue to fight this unseen war,
Hoping one day you'll find me worth more.
Worth more than the ghosts that haunt your mind,
More than the memories that bind.
Until then, I remain a silent plea,

Hoping someday you'll truly see.
That I'm not him, I'm someone new,
Desperate to build a future with you.

14. FOURTEENTH STITCH

You don't trust me at all,
Yet you tell me to trust you this time.
In the silence between your call,
I sense the echoes of your crime.
I told you that digging your past
Would tarnish the love we both claim.
You said, "Nothing will last
If trust isn't a part of the game."
And now you see,
It did affect our fragile tether.
It did increase your doubts in me,
And now we drift apart, untethered.
I suffer here, the blameless one,
Bearing sins of another's deeds.
Your battles fought, your wars not won,
Have planted in you mistrust's seeds.
I don't trust the word "trust" anymore,
It's fragile, shattered easily.
Its shards have cut us to the core,
A love now lost in misery.

In the shadows of our room,
Ghosts of your past, they linger near.
They weave a tapestry of gloom,
In every smile, in every tear.
Your eyes, they show a distant pain,
A hurt I can't make disappear.
Our love now seems a bitter chain,
Forged by each unspoken fear.
Promises, they weigh us down,
A burden on these weary hearts.
Each word, each sigh, a hollow sound,
As slowly, our togetherness departs.
The silence grows, a heavy shroud,
A chasm deep between our souls.
Where once our love was strong and proud,
Now trust is full of gaping holes.
In the stillness of the night,
I ponder if our love can stay.
Can hearts entwined in constant fight
Find solace in the light of day?
You don't trust me at all,
Yet you ask for faith anew.
But trust is like a fragile call,
That struggles in a world askew.
I don't trust the word "trust" anymore,
It's a vow too often broken.
Its pieces cut us to the core,

Leaving love a mere token.
Your past, a storm that haunts our skies,
Its rains have drenched our budding flame.
And as I look into your eyes,
I see the shadow of our blame.
The love we had now drifts apart,
Two souls adrift in seas of pain.
We grasp at straws with weary heart,
Yet trust eludes, and doubts remain.
You don't trust me at all,
Yet you seek my trust in kind.
But trust's a fortress, tall,
In ruins, with no peace to find.
In this tangled web of sorrow,
Our hearts seek a lost refrain.
Hoping for a bright tomorrow,
But bound by yesterday's chain.
I don't trust the word "trust" anymore,
It's a dream that's turned to dust.
In love's shadowed, endless war,
We've lost the sacred bond of trust.

15. FIFTEENTH STITCH

Now when I am done with everything,
I almost lost myself, the silent sting.
You came near, like a whisper in the night,
A ghost of love, in the pale moonlight.
Tears fell down through your cheeks on my palm,
A burning touch, no soothing balm.
Like concentrated sulfuric acid, they seared,
A pain so raw, the past appeared.
Our eyes met in that haunted space,
A silent conversation, an embrace.
Your lips trembled, words unspoken,
A fragile bond, almost broken.
As we exchanged breath, our worlds entwined,
In that moment, hearts unconfined.
I felt basorexia, an urge so deep,
A craving kiss, where shadows creep.
I pulled your chin up, eyes closed in trust,
In that fragile second, love robust.
Tasted those sweet lips of yours, again,
A mingled sorrow, a lover's bane.

Your scent, intoxicating, filled the air,
A fragrance of longing, love laid bare.
My heart raced, a wild, untamed beat,
In your arms, our worlds complete.
Fingers traced the contours of your face,
Each touch, a testament to grace.
Your skin, a canvas of stories told,
A history of love, in whispers bold.
We stood on the edge of a precipice,
A dance of desire, a lover's bliss.
In your embrace, the world faded away,
A timeless moment, where we lay.
Our bodies spoke in a language rare,
A symphony of passion, raw and bare.
Every touch, a note in love's song,
A melody where we both belong.
And forgave you for the very last time,
Our story written, in love's fleeting rhyme.
A final chapter, a bittersweet end,
Where hearts break, and souls transcend.
In that kiss, a world of pain released,
A moment of peace, our hearts appeased.
Yet, in the shadows of love's refrain,
Lingers the echo of a tender pain.
As dawn broke, and the night withdrew,
We stood apart, our bond anew.
In that fleeting moment, love's pure art,

A memory etched within the heart.
And so, with a heavy heart, I turned away,
A love once bright, now lost in the fray.
Yet, in the silence of the morning air,
Lingers the whisper of a love so rare.

16. SIXTEENTH STITCH

Even after all this,
You talked to him again...
You are still keeping connections,
As if our history was just a fleeting wind,
As if our love was just a lie.
I can't take this anymore,
The pain gnawing at my soul,
A relentless ache, an unending sorrow,
A wound that will never heal.
Tonight, you will lose me forever,
Not in the dramatic flare of a lover's quarrel,
But in the quiet surrender of a broken heart,
Crushed under the weight of betrayal.
I will drown myself in the abyss,
Of bottles and bitter oblivion,
And erase your memories from my life,
With each sip, with each tear.
I will become a ghost,
A shadow of what I once was,
A hollow shell, empty and devoid,

Of the warmth that you once kindled.
The nights will stretch endlessly,
In a cold and silent torment,
The echo of your laughter,
A haunting reminder of what once was.
But even in my numb despair,
The fragments of us will persist,
Like shards of glass in my mind,
Piercing and cutting with every breath.
I will try to forget,
But you will always linger,
A specter in the corners of my consciousness,
A wound that will never heal.
So tonight, I bid you farewell,
In the only way I know how,
By losing myself in the darkness,
And hoping it swallows me whole.
Even after all this,
You talked to him again...
You are still keeping connections,
And I am left to fade away,
Into the silence of my own despair.

17. SEVENTEENTH STITCH

I gave my all, but it was never enough,
In your eyes, my worth always too rough.
My heart was pure, my intentions true,
But I could never be loved by you.
Now, here I lie, on this cold, sterile bed,
Staring at the ceiling, wishing I were dead.
Counting the hours, till peace comes to me,
Longing for an end, from this misery.
Your absence is a dagger, sharp and cold,
No visits, no calls, no hand to hold.
All that they said, now echoes in my mind,
Your love was a lie, of the cruelest kind.
I poured my heart, my soul, into you,
Only to find your promises untrue.
My love, once a river, flowing free,
Now turned to hatred, a dark, stormy sea.
Admitted here, where the walls close in tight,
Your shadow lingers, a ghost in the night.
Not a glance, not a touch, not a word from you,
Your silence, the proof that our love was untrue.

Now, as I lie here, life slipping away,
I curse the day I fell for your sway.
For love, once a light, now a forbidden flame,
Burns my soul, as I wither in shame.
In the stillness of night, I hear whispers so low,
Memories of us, a cruel, haunting show.
Each moment we shared, now twisted and vile,
As I drown in despair, mile after mile.
The doctors and nurses, they come and they go,
Their faces a blur, their voices a woe.
They see not my heart, shattered and torn,
A soul left to die, so utterly forlorn.
Friends and family, they ask where you are,
Their pity, a knife, leaves a deep, festering scar.
I force a smile, say you're just busy today,
But inside, I'm crumbling, fading away.
The clock ticks loudly, a monotonous beat,
Marking the moments of my slow defeat.
Each second that passes, a weight on my chest,
Reminding me constantly, I'll never find rest.
In my dreams, I see you, but you're cold and aloof,
Your eyes, once warm, now a stark, bitter proof.
The love I believed in, a mere phantom, a wraith,
Mocking my trust, my once steadfast faith.
How did I become this shadow of sorrow,
Dreading each dawn, each empty tomorrow?
The bed feels like ice, the air like a tomb,

Trapped in this darkness, consumed by my gloom.
I reach for the phone, but my fingers retract,
What's the point in calling when you'll never act?
Your number, a lifeline that's tangled and frayed,
A symbol of hope that has cruelly decayed.
I wonder, did you ever care, even a bit?
Or was I a pawn in your game, just a misfit?
Your laughter, once music, now cuts like a blade,
Every sweet word, a bitter charade.
My breath grows shallow, my vision a blur,
The edges of life, beginning to stir.
In this final moment, a truth I've unearthed,
That love without honesty is of no worth.
In the end, I'll be free from this pain,
No more tears, no more love in vain.
Falling in love, a curse, a decree,
Never again, for it's prohibited for me.
So let the darkness take me, let it swallow me whole,
For I've nothing left, not even my soul.
The world grows distant, my body turns cold,
As I drift into silence, my story untold.
May my passing be gentle, my suffering cease,
In the arms of oblivion, I'll finally find peace.
And as I depart, one lesson remains,
That love, without truth, only deepens the stains.

18. 18TH STITCH, BUT THIS TIME WITH LOVE

I got 18 stitches on my leg,
And my 18th stitch is you.
Never thought someone would beg
To love me more than I ever knew.
Each stitch, a mark of pain endured,
A testament to battles fought and scars,
But you, my love, became my cure,
The light that heals from near and far.
All wounds are getting healed somehow,
By the ultimate stitch of love so true.
Thank you, "Rosogolla," now,
For showering all your care anew.
Before you, days were cloaked in shadows,
Nights haunted by the ghosts of yore.
Each scar a reminder of past sorrows,
Yet your love showed me there's so much more.
You came like hope, a whisper of light,
Like dawn breaking the longest night.

Your love, a salve to my weary sight,
Made my heart soar to new heights.
With every touch, with every kiss,
You mend the broken parts of me.
Your presence is pure, eternal bliss,
A reminder of love's true decree.
In your eyes, I see my reflection clear,
A version I thought lost in time.
Your love breathed life into my fear,
Turning my pain into rhyme.
You taught me that staying and loving back
Someone who truly loves you is a gift.
With you, there's no love that I lack,
Together, we rise, together, we lift.
Thank you, "Rosogolla," for being my stitch,
For being the love I never knew I sought.
Your care is my treasure, a perfect pitch,
With you, my battles are fought and won.
In the darkest hours, when shadows loom,
Your light broke through, a guiding moon.
You are the sun that dispels all gloom,
In your embrace, my heart's tune.
The past now fades, a distant song,
As you step forward, my guiding star.
Your love is my strength, forever long,
With you, I know just who we are.

Your laughter, a melody that heals,
Your touch, a caress so true.
In your arms, my sanctuary feels
Like home, where dreams come through.
All these 18 stitches made me see
The true value of love so pure.
They taught me that every scar can be
A story of courage, of love's allure.
You are the stitch that made me whole,
The final thread in my life's weave.
With you, I am strong, body and soul,
Ready to love, ready to believe.
So here's to the stitches, to our quest,
To the love that binds and sets us free.
In your arms, I find my rest,
In your heart, my eternity.
Thank you, my love, for all you give,
For every moment, touch, and rhyme.
You are my ultimate reason to live,
Grateful for you, now and for all time.
Together, we weave a tale so sweet,
One of love, of healing, of endless skies.
With you, my world feels complete,
And the stitches fade as love's light flies.